THE LAST RIVER

JOHN WESLEY POWELL &
THE COLORADO RIVER EXPLORING EXPEDITION

FOR PETER AND YURI

Editor: Elizabeth Mann
Design: Lesley Ehlers Design

Library of Congress Cataloging-in-Publication Data

Waldman, Stuart, 1941-
    The Last River: John Wesley Powell & the Colorado River Exploring Expedition/ by
Stuart Waldman ; illustrated by Gregory Manchess.
        p. cm. — (A great explorers book)
    Includes bibliographical references and index
    ISBN 1-931414-09-2
    1. Powell, John Wesley, 1834-1902—Juvenile literature. 2 Explorers—West
(U.S.)—Biography—Juvenile literature. 3. Colorado River (Colo.–Mexico—Discovery and
exploration—Juvenile literature. 4 West (U.S.)—Discovery and exploration—Juvenile
literature. 1. Manchess, Gregory, ill. ll. Title. lll. Series

    F788. P88W35 2005
    550.92—dc22
    [B]
                                                                            2005041580

Photograph Page 11: Library of Congress
Photographs Pages 7, 21, 24, 30: United States Geological Survey

Printed in China

JOHN WESLEY POWELL

**KEEP THE OTHER SIDE
OF THIS PAGE OPEN.**

☞

**YOU CAN READ ABOUT
POWELL'S TRAVELS
AND FOLLOW THEM ON THE
MAP AT THE SAME TIME.**

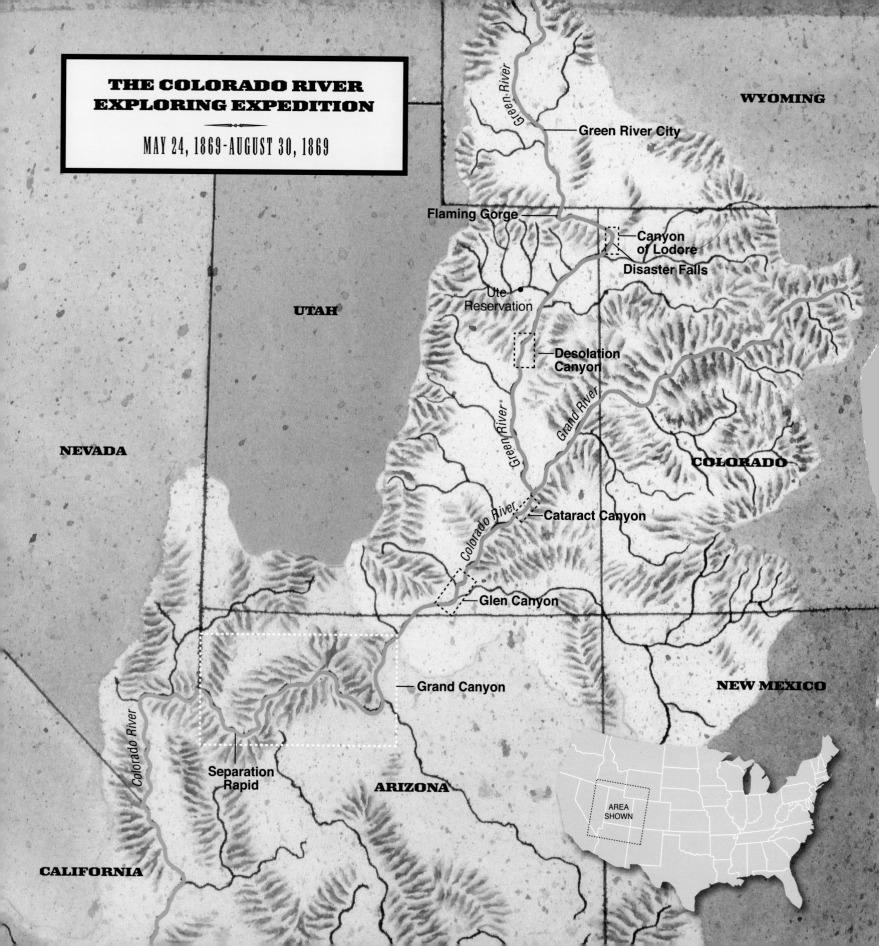

THE COLORADO RIVER EXPLORING EXPEDITION

MAY 24, 1869-AUGUST 30, 1869

WYOMING

Green River

Green River City

Flaming Gorge

Canyon of Lodore

Disaster Falls

Ute Reservation

Desolation Canyon

UTAH

Green River

Grand River

COLORADO

NEVADA

Colorado River

Cataract Canyon

Glen Canyon

Grand Canyon

NEW MEXICO

Colorado River

Separation Rapid

CALIFORNIA

ARIZONA

AREA SHOWN

Each spring, the snowpack melted on the peaks of the Wind River mountain range in Wyoming. Icy water trickled into thousands of small streams that joined together to become the Green River. It snaked its way south into Utah where it merged with the Grand River flowing down from the Rockies. The joining of these two powerful mountain rivers unleashed a violent torrent of rushing water. It was called the Colorado River.

From its sources more than 14,000 feet above sea level to its mouth in the desert lowlands, the Colorado dropped nearly three miles! It gained speed and power on its downhill journey and flowed through hundreds of miles of deep canyons. The force of the water squeezing into the narrow canyons kicked up high waves. During storms, the Colorado flooded and gouged out chunks of the canyons' walls. Boulders bounced into the water like beach balls, settling in the riverbed. Waves slammed against the boulders and ricocheted back, breaking wildly, unpredictably, in all directions at once. At times, the swirling currents formed whirlpools that could suck a boat in.

These were the rapids of the Colorado, and they were so terrifying that few people, even the native tribes that had lived near the river for a thousand years, dared to put their boats in it.

THE LAST RIVER

JOHN WESLEY POWELL &
THE COLORADO RIVER EXPLORING EXPEDITION

BY STUART WALDMAN

ILLUSTRATED BY GREGORY MANCHESS

MIKAYA PRESS

NEW YORK

The land the Colorado flowed through was a vast, empty desert. Water was scarce, game was sparse, and there was little vegetation. Spanish conquistadors discovered the Colorado in 1541, but finding no gold, they ignored it. In the 19th century, American trappers explored some of the Colorado's tributary rivers in search of beaver, and Mormon settlers built towns nearby, but the Colorado itself defied exploration.

By the time of the Civil War, most of the river and a large swath of land around it appeared on American maps as a blank space. It was the only unmapped territory and the last unexplored river in the United States. There was every reason to believe it would remain that way.

ON THE MORNING OF MAY 24, 1869, the entire population of Green River City gathered at the riverbank to watch the Colorado River Exploring Expedition begin its journey. It was not a large crowd. Green River City had been founded just months before, and contained only a few small buildings, a train station and a store that also served as a saloon. The expedition's crew had spent the previous night in that saloon celebrating with the townspeople.

An American flag was raised in the lead boat. The people waved and cheered. The expedition's leader, John Wesley Powell, tipped his hat to the crowd and they cheered again. Powell gave a signal and the four boats pushed off. Minutes later they disappeared around a bend in the river.

The rest of the country was not as enthusiastic as the people of Green River City. Few had heard of the Colorado River Exploring Expedition, and of those that had, few believed it would succeed. John Wesley Powell wasn't an explorer; he was a college professor. He had never piloted a boat through a canyon rapid, much less a rapid of the Colorado. He was small, a little over 5'6" tall, and he weighed only 120 pounds. Most improbable of all, the man who was leading an expedition down the most dangerous river in America had only one arm.

John Wesley Powell was born in 1834 and raised in the Midwest, the son of a farmer. When he was 12, his father told him he had to quit school and help run the farm. Wes, as his family called him, loved books and learning. He read in the morning in the fields. He read in the wagon while hauling goods to market. He read late at night in the quiet of the barn. By the time he was 21, Powell had learned enough to pass an entrance exam and enroll in college.

He was fascinated by geology, the study of the earth and its origins. It was a new science and few colleges taught it. Once again Powell became his own instructor. He read every geology text he could get his hands on and then went beyond books. During vacations, he trekked through wilderness areas, studying the landscape and collecting rocks, minerals and fossils. One summer, Powell rowed a small wooden boat down the length of the Mississippi River, over 2,000 miles, by himself!

Powell looked forward to these solitary expeditions, and not only for the science. He loved the challenges of the wild. What was around the bend in the river? How far to the top of the mountain? What was on the other side? He called the difficulties and dangers "adventure" and he craved it as much as he craved knowledge.

By 1860, the boy who had left school at 12 was teaching science, lecturing on geology, and running a small natural history museum filled with the thousands of fossils he collected on his expeditions. A year later, the Civil War broke out.

Powell enlisted as a private in the Union army. His first battle was one of the war's most terrible: Shiloh, where more than 20,000 soldiers were killed or wounded in just two days. A bullet shattered Powell's wrist and an infection spread up his right arm. To save his life, the arm had to be amputated just below the elbow.

During the Civil War, surgery took place in dimly lit, unsanitary tents like these. Overworked surgeons had to operate on thousands of men during battles like Shiloh. Speed was essential and limbs were amputated in as little as six minutes! Powell's arm never healed properly and he was in pain for the rest of his life.

He spent nearly a year recuperating, nursed by Emma Dean Powell, who he had married the year before. Although he could have gone home, Powell rejoined the army and fought for the next three years, rising to the rank of major.

When the war ended in 1865, Powell was a 31-year-old, one-armed man, with a wife and no job. His father gave him some advice: "Wes, you are a maimed man. Settle down at teaching. It's a noble profession. Get this nonsense of science and adventure out of your mind."

He tried. Powell became a professor of science at Illinois Wesleyan College. He enjoyed teaching and was one of the school's more popular professors. But something was missing. In the summer of 1867, he organized his first geological expedition since before the war. Along with Emma Dean, his brother Walter, and ten students and friends, Powell traveled to America's western territories to study the geology of the Rocky Mountains.

The trip changed John Wesley Powell's life—or rather it gave him back his life. He may have been a "maimed man," but as he led the way up icy trails to the tallest peaks in the Rockies, he discovered that he was as capable as ever in the wild. His love of the outdoors and adventure returned in a rush. Before the expedition was over, Powell was planning the next one.

His guide in the Rockies, a trapper named Jack Sumner, had spoken to Powell about an unexplored river that flowed through canyons so deep they were shrouded in darkness. As a geologist, Powell knew that such canyons were created over millions of years and contained ancient rocks and fossils. On maps, he saw the serpentine line of the Colorado River abruptly end in a blank space. Mysterious canyons, a geologic treasure, an unmapped river, the last unexplored territory in the United States! It was all irresistible to a man like John Wesley Powell.

By the next summer, he was back in the Rockies planning a route and looking for a crew for what he called the Colorado River Exploring Expedition. Although it was to be a scientific expedition, Powell wasn't looking for scientists. He would study the geology of the Colorado's canyons. The crew's job would be to get him there.

The first person who signed on was Jack Sumner. Like Powell, Sumner had grown up on a farm and left as soon as he was old enough. Moving to the Rockies, he became a trader, trapper, professional hunter and guide. Sumner developed a reputation as a man who could be relied on not only for his skill and knowledge, but also for his fearlessness. He once snowshoed across the Rocky Mountains in the dead of winter!

Four of Sumner's friends joined the expedition with him.

Bill Dunn, with hair that flowed nearly to his waist, an unkempt beard almost as long, and a single, greasy buckskin outfit, was an old-time "mountain man" come to life. Like the famous trappers who had explored the West decades before, Dunn knew how to follow uncharted trails, hunt for his own food, go for months without sleeping in a bed, and survive under conditions that few people could or would tolerate.

Billy Hawkins was a tough 21-year-old who had lied about his age in order to fight in the Union army when he was 15. Although usually friendly and cheerful, Hawkins was rumored to be in trouble with the law.

Oramel Howland at 36 was the oldest man on the expedition and the most educated of the westerners. Powell would give him one of the expedition's most complicated and important tasks: drawing the first complete maps of the Colorado River and its canyons. Seneca Howland, Oramel's younger brother, joined the expedition along with him.

Over the coming months, Powell recruited three more men. He found Sergeant George Bradley at an army fort. Bradley had gone to sea as a young man and knew how to handle and repair boats. Powell was so eager to have him in the crew that he wrote to the man he had served under at Shiloh, General Ulysses S. Grant, and got Bradley an early discharge from the army.

THE JOURNAL OF JACK SUMNER

Heretofore, all attempts in exploring the Colorado of the West, throughout its entire course have been miserable failures. Whether our attempt will turn out the same time alone will show. If we fail it will not be for the want of a complete outfit of material and men used to hardships.

Powell found 19-year-old Andy Hall on the Green River rowing a boat he'd built himself. Hall had lived on his own from the age of 14 and had guided cavalry troops through Indian territory.

Frank Goodman found Powell. He was a young Englishman who had read of America's Wild West and crossed the Atlantic looking for adventure. He met Powell in Green River City, and upon hearing about his dangerous expedition, pleaded for a chance to come along. Powell, perhaps thinking Goodman's enthusiasm would make up for his lack of experience, made him a crew member.

Finally there was Walter Powell. John Wesley Powell had praised his younger brother's coolness and courage during the Rocky Mountain expedition, but there was a dark and tragic side to Walter that he didn't talk about. Walter Powell had been captured by Confederate troops during the Civil War and imprisoned in one of the South's most notorious camps. Hundreds of men were jammed into small stockades and made to stand in the sun all day with little food and water. At night they lay on the cold, bare earth, the stench of the dead and dying filling their nostrils. Walter Powell survived but never truly recovered from the horrors of his prison experience. Once friendly and outgoing, he had become sullen, depressed and given to sudden violent outbursts.

With his crew set, Powell went east to buy boats. Choosing them would be as crucial as choosing the crew, and even more difficult. Since nobody had gone through the Colorado's rapids, there was no way of knowing what kind of boat would perform best. Powell believed that the most important thing was to get through the rapids as quickly as possible, so he bought boats designed for speed. Called Whitehalls—after the street in New York City where they were first built—their sleek, curvy bottoms glided swiftly through water. Whitehalls were so fast they were used by New York's harbor police to chase thieves escaping by boat.

Powell had special cargo compartments built into the boats. These would hold guns and ammunition for hunting, spare clothes, scientific instruments and thousands of pounds of flour, bacon and dried fruits.

It had taken nearly a year of planning, but by the beginning of May, everything was ready. The boats were put on the new Trans-Continental Railroad and shipped to Green River City. Powell had decided to begin his expedition on the Green River because there was no railroad station near the Colorado. The crew would have had to have hauled the boats hundreds of miles by wagon over steep, rugged mountain trails. Instead, they carried the boats just a few hundred feet from the Green River City station to the Green River. From there, they would row down to the Colorado.

While the route was easier, it was still dangerous. With its own deep canyons and wild rapids, the Green River was nearly as deadly as the Colorado. Mountain men had explored different parts of it, but nobody had been able to navigate its entire length.

Despite its reputation, the first week on the Green was like a holiday. The boats moved lazily along broad open waters. Each afternoon the men camped on sandy beaches shaded by leafy cottonwood trees. They hunted ducks on the river and wild sheep in the hills. They gawked like sightseers at the red sandstone walls of Flaming Gorge, the Green's first canyon. Wild grapevines trailed along the riverbank. Flocks of geese paddled gently in the still water. And there wasn't a rapid in sight.

Flaming Gorge

As the boats left Flaming Gorge, the men heard the faint hiss of rushing water. They rowed toward the entrance to the next canyon and the sound became louder. Inside, the hiss turned to a roar that echoed off the cliffs. The peaceful Green erupted into white-foamed waves.

The four boats went single file, with Sumner and Bill Dunn rowing the lead boat, the *Emma Dean*. They removed their boots, ready to be tossed in the river at any moment. Like all rowers, Sumner and Dunn faced backwards, making it difficult for them to see the rocks up ahead. John Wesley Powell was their eyes. He stood in the front of the *Emma Dean*, holding on to a strap for balance like a rodeo rider on a bucking horse. He scanned the water for a safe path and shouted directions to Sumner and Dunn. As the *Emma Dean* zig-zagged between rocks, the three other boats—*Maid of the Canyon*, *No Name* and *Kitty Clyde's Sister* (named after a popular song)— trailed behind like ducklings following their mother. In a few minutes, all were in calm water. They had run their first canyon rapid and had barely gotten wet.

The next morning they rowed toward another rapid, one that seemed far more dangerous. The river dove downwards like a waterslide, a slide roiling with waves and dotted with jagged rocks. Powell ordered the *Emma Dean* to shore. Standing on the riverbank, he looked down the "drop." He declared it too dangerous to run and told the men to "line" the boats.

They unloaded the cargo and piled it on shore. They tied ropes to the front and back of the *Emma Dean*. One of the men anchored the front line to a rock on the riverbank at the bottom of the drop. Using the back lines, the rest of the crew carefully guided the boat out into the rapid and slowly down the drop. The force of falling water pushed at the *Emma Dean*. The men pulled the ropes as if they were in a tug of war against the river. At one point the boat came close to a rock and one of the men had to push it away with an oar. Finally, when the *Emma Dean* was clear of all obstacles, and near the bottom of the drop, they let go. The man stationed below grabbed the front line and pulled it to shore.

When they had finished lining all four boats, the crew had to move the tons of cargo scattered along the riverbank. Weighed down like pack animals, they carried sacks of food, boxes of instruments, gun crates, tents, blankets and spare clothes down to where the boats were tied up. They made dozens of trips, back and forth, and when they were finished, they began reloading the cargo compartments. Lining took hours and was tedious and exhausting, but it was a safe way to get past a dangerous drop.

The next day the unpredictable river changed yet again. There were fewer rocks and broader, more open channels, and the boats ran dozens of rapids. During one stretch, Powell estimated they were moving down the river at 60 miles an hour! It was the opposite of lining and the crew loved it. There could be no greater thrill than skimming the waves, riding a roller coaster of foam, shouting whoops of joy over the rapids' roar, and finally making it to calm water—wet, bedraggled and giddy with victory.

With each new rapid, the crew gained in confidence and skill, but the boats didn't perform nearly as well. Whitehalls were designed for the quiet waters of New York's sheltered harbor, not the Colorado's churning rapids. Waves swept over the Whitehalls and water poured in, making the boats heavier and rowing more difficult. In a rapid with few rocks to maneuver around, this was little more than an annoyance. In a dangerous rapid, this could cause serious problems— as they were soon to discover.

On June 7, the boats approached the entrance to a canyon with extremely tall and narrow cliffs. Sunlight made it down to the river only a few hours a day. The men named it the Canyon of Lodore, after a dark and gloomy castle in an old English poem.

Once inside, the *Emma Dean* faced a series of steep drops choked with boulders. Powell had Bill Dunn wave a flag, signalling the boats to shore. Oramel Howland, who was piloting the *No Name*, didn't see the flag, and the boat was caught in a rapid with extremely high waves. Water rose quickly inside the boat. The heavy Whitehall lumbered in the churning water, impossible to steer. It whirled helplessly down the drop and smashed sideways into a large boulder. The *No Name* broke apart.

The Howland brothers and Frank Goodman held tight to a part of the wreckage. It carried them down the river, speeding toward another menacing drop. As they passed a small sandbar, all three men let go and swam towards it. The Howlands made it, but Frank Goodman disappeared beneath the waves. He popped up seconds later, gagging on river water, his hands clutching a small rock. The waves pummeled him. It was only a matter of time before he would be dragged under again, perhaps for good.

Oramel Howland waded as far into the rapid as he dared and held out a long driftwood branch. Goodman pushed off from the rock, swam a few feet and grabbed the branch. Oramel pulled him to safety.

The Canyon of Lodore

Meanwhile, the crew lined the *Emma Dean* down the drop and slid it into the river. Jack Sumner leaped into the boat, rowed to the sandbar and rescued the men.

They named the rapid Disaster Falls. The expedition had lost a boat and its cargo, including thousands of pounds of food. They also lost a crew member. Frank Goodman decided he had found a little too much adventure in the West. When the expedition stopped near a trading post on a Ute Indian Reservation, Goodman told Powell he was leaving.

It was the last chance to turn back. From this point on, they would not be near trading posts, reservations, towns or people. They were entering the desert. The boats drifted into a canyon where the temperature reached over a 100 degrees during the day and a hot sand-filled wind swept through the camp at night. The men called it Desolation Canyon.

Desolation Canyon

Lining felt like torture in the heat. If it had been up to the crew, they would have run even the most dangerous drops. As leader, Powell had to be more cautious. If a man were injured, it would be impossible to get help in the desert. Running rapids also endangered the food supply. Water seeped into the cargo compartments. Slabs of bacon had turned rancid and sacks of flour had become soggy lumps. Added to what had been lost in the *No Name*, half the expedition's food was gone. Each rapid they ran made the situation worse.

Despite his battles with the river, Powell never forgot that he was leading a scientific expedition. He climbed the walls of almost every new canyon to study its geology and collect its rocks and fossils. Dunn or Bradley carried the instruments used to calculate a canyon's height. Oramel Howland sometimes came along with a sketch pad so he could draw his map from the top of the canyon.

There were no trails on the nearly perpendicular walls. The men had no special equipment to help them climb, and their leather boots had become worn and frayed from the water. It was hard, slow, one foot after another, rock-by-rock, climbing.

THE JOURNAL OF GEORGE BRADLEY

We camp tonight at the head of one that Major has concluded we cannot run. . . . I should run it if left to myself as the only trouble is sunken rocks, and in such swift water any rock that would injure us would show itself and we could avoid it. The Major's way is safe but I as a lazy man look to the ease of the thing.

On July 8, Powell and Bradley were 800 feet above Desolation Canyon's floor. Powell grabbed a rock above him, pulled himself up, and found a ledge for one foot. He probed with his other foot but could find no place for it. A man with two arms would have simply held on to the rock with one hand, grabbed a second rock with the other hand and searched for a new foothold. Powell couldn't. He was stuck.

Bradley was too far above Powell to reach him. There were no tree branches on Desolation's bare cliffs so Bradley used the only thing he had. He took off his long underwear and lowered it to Powell. Pressing his body against the wall, Powell let go of the rock and flailed at a pant leg hovering above him. He grabbed it and Bradley hauled him up, as Powell held tight with his one hand and swayed 800 feet above the canyon floor. When he got to Bradley's ledge, the two men continued climbing as if it nothing had happened, as if it were all in a day's work. And for these men, it was.

JOHN WESLEY POWELL

THE EXPLORATION OF THE COLORADO RIVER AND ITS CANYONS

Among these rocks, in chutes, whirlpools and great waves, with rushing breakers and foam, the water finds its way, still tumbling down. . . . A very hard day's work has been done, and at evening I sit on a rock by the edge of the river and look at the water and listen to its roar. . . . Darkness is coming on; but the waves are rolling with crests of foam so white they seem to almost give a light of their own.

On July 16, the expedition reached the junction of the Green and Grand Rivers. They had made it to the Colorado River, but they were far too busy to celebrate. The Colorado's first canyon had so many drops that the men named it Cataract, another word for waterfall. They lined many of them, but even those they ran were clogged with rocks. Since Disaster Falls, the men had become more experienced in steering waterlogged Whitehalls, but Cataract Canyon's rapids gave them all they could handle. Time after time, the boats sideswiped boulders whose jagged edges tore into the wood. The boats began to leak. John Wesley and Walter Powell climbed Cataract's 1,500-foot cliffs and collected the sticky resinous sap called pitch from dwarf pine trees. The men spread the pitch over the leaks, making the boats watertight—at least until the next rapid.

The lush valleys of the Green River had provided plenty of game, but in the desert they could go for days without seeing an animal. The Colorado was teeming with fish, but it also had an abundance of insects. The fish ignored hooks baited with soggy bread and went instead for the tasty flies that lay atop the water.

The men's survival now depended on the food stored in the cargo compartments, but as Cataract's rapids filled the boats with water, the food spoiled at an alarming rate. Powell had no choice but to ration. An exhausting day on the river was rewarded with smaller and smaller portions.

In the beginning, the men joked about their situation. After a particularly sparse dinner, Billy Hawkins asked Powell for his instruments so he could find the latitude of the nearest pie.

When the jokes stopped, the grumbling began. Much of it was about Powell. He bought the wrong kind of boats. He hadn't brought enough food. He wasted time collecting rocks and fossils. Some of this complaining was harmless, a way to let off steam. But Powell often made things worse. He could be harsh with the men, believing the expedition needed the firm discipline of a military operation to succeed. Powell expected to be called "Major," and would issue commands as if he were still in the army. He even ate his meals separately from the men, as army officers did.

The westerners in particular rankled at such treatment. They were proud men whose life in the wilderness had given them a sense of freedom and independence. They acknowledged that it was Powell's expedition, but they weren't in the army and they didn't like being ordered around.

Walter Powell added to his brother's problems. He rarely spoke to any of the crew, and when he did he was often nasty. The crew tried their best to ignore Walter, but it wasn't easy.

LETTER FROM BILLY HAWKINS

None of the party except the Major liked Captain [Walter] Powell. He had a bullying way about him that was not then practiced in the west. He threatened to slap me several times for trying to sing as he did.

Glen Canyon

The men put their complaints in their journals and letters but didn't confront John Wesley Powell directly. The problems remained below the surface, like rocks hidden in a rapid.

When the turmoil of Cataract Canyon gave way to the calm of Glen Canyon, the mood brightened—at least temporarily. The days were still searingly hot, but the river was gentle and Glen Canyon was extraordinarily beautiful. Its walls were striated with layers of red, orange, purple, brown and yellow sandstone and were carved into a fairyland of wondrous forms: high, graceful arches, twisting towers, mossy coves and hidden grottos.

At one bend of the river, the men hiked through a grove of cottonwood trees and entered an enormous cavern. The ceiling vaulted as high as a church steeple. A small opening cut through the rock and brought a shaft of light down from the of top the canyon more than a thousand feet above. They made camp there that night. As the light from their fire flickered off the multi-colored stone, Walter Powell serenaded the crew. The men named the cavern Music Temple.

Glen Canyon was the last peaceful part of the journey. On August 3, the expedition entered the canyon that Powell called the Great Unknown. Although native tribes were quite familiar with it, and one, the Havusapi, even lived along its cliffs, the Grand Canyon had been seen by few other Americans. One thing was certain: it dwarfed by far all the other canyons of the Colorado. The Grand Canyon was estimated go for hundreds of miles. In places it was so wide that from its rim the other side appeared a distant shore and so deep the Colorado looked like a peaceful mountain stream.

It wasn't. The Colorado River was at its most dangerous in the Grand Canyon. A spider's web of side creeks flowed into the Grand Canyon and their currents clashed with the Colorado, creating powerful and unpredictable waves. During floods, boulders rolled through dozens of side canyons and dropped down into the Grand Canyon. The boulders piled in high mounds and produced the most perilous drops on the Colorado River. The men no longer gloried in the thrill of running the rapids. In the Grand Canyon it was grim, hard, frightening work.

JOHN WESLEY POWELL

THE EXPLORATION OF THE COLORADO RIVER AND ITS CANYONS

We are now ready to start on our way down the Great Unknown. . . . We have an unknown distance to run, an unknown river to explore. What falls there are, we know not; what rocks beset the channel we know not; what walls rise over the river, we know not. Ah well, we may conjecture many things. The men talk as cheerfully as ever; jests are bandied about freely this morning; but to me the cheer is somber and the jests are ghastly.

The riverbed contained a clay-like sediment called silt. It saturated the Colorado giving it a distinctive reddish color, and its name. The Spanish called it Rio Colorado—The Red River.

JOHN WESLEY POWELL

THE EXPLORATION OF THE COLORADO RIVER AND ITS CANYONS

I climb so high that the men and boats are lost in the black depths below and the dashing river is a rippling brook, and still there is more canyon above than below. All about me are interesting geologic records. The book is open and I can read as I run. All about me are grand views, too, for the clouds are playing again in the gorges. But somehow I think of the nine days rations and the bad river. . . .

When it rained, silt poured down from side canyons, splattering the boats and the men. Yet when the sun appeared, the 115-degree heat made them long for the rain. There was no relief at night. It was difficult to find a good campsite, and some nights the men slept squeezed between boulders while the rain poured down on them.

August 15 was a typical day in the Grand Canyon. The *Emma Dean* slammed into a boulder and began leaking. The *Maid of the Canyon* was caught in whirlpools and spun through the rapid like a wobbly top. And Oramel Howland's hand-drawn map of the Grand Canyon, which was so important to the expedition's scientific mission, washed overboard and was lost.

John Wesley Powell was frustrated. He was in a geological wonderland, filled with the some of the oldest exposed rocks on the North American continent. He should have spent months poring over every nook and cranny, but he didn't have months, or weeks. He barely had days. With the food nearly gone, the expedition had to keep moving. Otherwise, they would all starve.

Trapped by the Grand Canyon's towering walls, in a prison of heat, hunger and misery, the trouble between Powell and the crew burst into the open.

It began when Bill Dunn fell in the water while carrying one of Powell's instruments in his pocket. It was ruined and the Major exploded. He ordered Dunn to pay for the expensive instrument or leave the expedition right then.

It was an impossible demand and the men were astonished. Except for Walter Powell, the entire crew rallied behind Dunn. Sumner confronted Powell and told him his orders could not and would not be obeyed. Bradley, Hall and Hawkins threatened to leave with Dunn. In the end, Powell backed down, but bad feelings lingered on both sides.

A few days later, Dunn and Powell got into another argument. Powell cursed Dunn, and Dunn called him a cripple. An enraged Walter Powell charged at Dunn. Billy Hawkins jumped on Walter and threw him into the river. Walter threatened to shoot both Dunn and Hawkins. Eventually, the men were separated without anyone being hurt.

There were no more incidents, but the damage had been done. Up to that point, the men may have resented Powell, but they never questioned that he was the leader. That was no longer the case.

By August 26, Powell believed they were close to the end of the expedition. Beyond the Grand Canyon, the Colorado had been mapped and explored, and there were settlements with people and food.

As if to mock his hopes, the next day Powell looked down at the worst rapids he'd seen on the entire voyage. The Grand Canyon was only 50 feet wide at that point and the riverbed was choked with rocks. There were two steep drops that churned with violent waves. If the boats made it down the drops, through the waves and around the rocks, they'd still have to get past a large granite outcrop that jutted from the right bank and blocked half the river. The cliffs were nearly sheer, making lining difficult if not impossible.

Powell inspected the rapid from every angle. He thought he saw a way to line the boats at least down the first drop. He also spotted a narrow but rock-free channel through the second drop. After that, if they rowed hard, they might maneuver around the boulders and get by the outcrop.

He told the men they would run the rapid in the morning.

That night, Oramel Howland took Powell aside and told him that it was impossible to run the rapid. Before the fights, Howland might have offered his opinion but left it to Powell to make the final decision. Now what the Major wanted meant little to him. He informed Powell that no matter what anyone else did, he, his brother Seneca and Bill Dunn had decided to climb out of the Grand Canyon and walk to the nearest settlement.

While Howland slept, Powell, using an instrument called a sextant, calculated his location. It confirmed what he had suspected: they would be out of the Grand Canyon in a matter of days. He then went over Howland's plan. After climbing out of the Grand Canyon, he estimated that they would be at least 75 miles from a settlement. It was all desert, but it had rained more than usual, and there might be pools of water in the sand. Still, nine starving men might not have the strength to make it.

Powell wavered. Should they face the rapids or the desert? In the morning, he brought the crew together and discussed the options. Walter Powell left the decision to his brother. Hawkins and Hall, the youngest and wildest, said they would take on the rapid. But so did the older Bradley and the experienced Sumner. That decided it for Powell. The expedition would finish the way it had started: on the river.

THE JOURNAL OF GEORGE BRADLEY

There is discontent in camp tonight and I fear some of the party will take to the mountains but hope not. This is decidedly the darkest day of the trip but I don't despair. I shall be one to try and run it rather than take to the mountains.

LETTER FROM BILLY HAWKINS

Dunn held me by the hand and tears came into his eyes as he said he hated to leave Sumner and me, that we had many a hard and daring time together before we ever saw the Colorado River. "But," he said, "Billy you cannot blame me." I could not answer. For once in my life I was hurt to the very heart...

Only two boats were needed to carry the remaining six men. The *Emma Dean*, badly battered, was left behind tied to a rock. With Dunn and the Howlands helping, the men lined the boats down the first drop.

All that remained was to say good-bye. It was a difficult moment for everyone. The men had lived together for more than three months. They had faced danger together and depended on each other for their lives. Now, so close to their goal, the expedition had split apart. Tears welled in the eyes of men who prided themselves on their toughness. George Bradley broke down and wept.

Oramel and Seneca Howland and Bill Dunn looked on as the six men got in their boats and pushed off into the river.

The boats hugged the canyon wall. The *Maid of the Canyon* scraped against one large boulder but remained upright. As both boats plunged down the second drop, waves battered them from all sides. Rowing was useless. They put their oars in the boat and held on. Somehow they made it to the bottom of the drop but the boats were so full of water they were half-submerged.

The men took their oars and rowed with all their strength, picking their way through the minefield of boulders until, with a final hard pull to the left, they swung around the giant outcrop. Suddenly all was calm and quiet. It had taken less than a minute to run the rapid.

They turned and saw their friends struggling up the the Grand Canyon's enormous cliffs. Oramel Howland, Seneca Howland and Bill Dunn were never seen again.

JOHN WESLEY POWELL

THE EXPLORATION OF THE COLORADO RIVER AND ITS CANYONS

*Now the danger is over; now the toil is ceased; now the gloom has disappeared; now the firmament is bounded only by the horizan; and what a vast expanse of stars can be seen!
The river rolls by in silent majesty; the quiet of the camp is sweet; our joy is almost ecstasy.*

The two boats continued down the river. By the next afternoon, the water was calm and the cliffs no longer loomed above them. They were out of the Grand Canyon. The Colorado River Exploring Expedition had come to an end.

The men sat by the campfire talking late into the night. Bradley's thoughts were with his three friends, alone somewhere in the desert. The practical Sumner calculated how many miles they had made that day (42 1/2). Powell thought of all they had gone through since leaving Green River City, and compared it to the most difficult time in his life, seven years before, as he lay near death in a hospital tent at Shiloh.

Now, sitting beneath a dome of stars, far from the dangers of the Grand Canyon, the fear and anxiety were gone. They had done it!

The following morning they met a group of Mormon pioneers and were soon gorging on fish, squash and fresh melons. Two weeks later, Powell was in a Chicago hotel giving interviews to a large group of reporters. The story of the men who had come out of the Grand Canyon like ghosts, and the one-armed professor who led them, had created a sensation. John Wesley Powell became known as "the conqueror of the Colorado," America's newest hero.

He wasn't finished. Over the next decade, Powell helped organize a series of scientific expeditions to the Colorado and its canyons. Geologists, surveyors and mapmakers swarmed through the area. In 1880, the first geological study of the Grand Canyon was completed. It found that its most ancient rocks were nearly two billion years old!

In 1882, the map of the United States had no blank spaces.

AFTER

ORAMEL HOWLAND, SENECA HOWLAND AND BILL DUNN: When he returned to the Colorado a year later, Powell was told that the three men had been murdered by Indians of the Shivwits tribe. But many people, including Jack Sumner and Bill Hawkins didn't believe it. The Shivwits had always been known as a peaceful tribe. As westerners, both Sumner and Hawkins knew that it wasn't unusual for Indians to be blamed for crimes that others had committed.

Although their bodies were never found, it seems certain Oramel and Seneca Howland and Bill Dunn died somewhere in the desert. Whether they were murdered, and if so, who did it and why, remains a mystery to this day. ✸

GEORGE BRADLEY settled in California where he ran a small ranch. He became seriously ill in 1885, and moved back to Newbury, Massachusetts, where he was born. His sisters took care of him until he died that that same year at the age of 50. ✸

FRANK GOODMAN became the westerner he had dreamed of being. He lived, at various times, in Colorado, Wyoming, Utah and Arizona, working as a hunter, trapper and sheep rancher. He married, raised six children and died in 1915 at the age of 71. ✸

ANDY HALL moved to Arizona where he rode shotgun on Wells Fargo stage coaches. In August of 1882, he was killed during a robbery. He was 32 years old. ✸

BILLY HAWKINS also settled in Arizona. Besides farming and raising six sons, the man once rumored to be an outlaw served as Justice of the Peace. He died in 1919 at the age of 71, the last surviving member of the Colorado River Exploring Expedition. ❧

WALTER POWELL'S sisters took care of him for much of his life, but his mental condition continued to deteriorate. Eventually, he was committed to an asylum where he died in 1915, at the age of 72. ❧

JOHN WESLEY POWELL moved to Washington, D.C., where he became the director of the United States Geological Survey, the government agency responsible for mapping the United States. He was also one of the founders of the National Geographic Society and the Smithsonian Museum's Bureau of Ethnology, which studied the languages and cultures of the Native American tribes. Powell died in 1902 at the age of 68. ❧

JACK SUMNER moved to California after the Colorado River Exploring Expedition. In 1871, he returned to the Rockies, traveling alone on horseback through the scorching heat of Death Valley. Although he married and had three sons, Sumner never gave up his adventurous life working as a hunter, trapper and gold propector. He died in Utah in 1907 at the age of 67. ❧

SOURCES

Bennett, Jeff, *The Complete Whitewater Rafter*, Ragged Mountain Press: Camden, 1996.

Darrah, William Culp, *Powell of the Colorado*, Princeton University Press: Princeton, 1951.

Dolnick, Edward, *Down the Great Unknown: John Wesley Powell's 1869 Journey of Discovery and Tragedy Through the Grand Canyon*, HarperCollins, New York, 2001.

Fradkin, Phillip L., *The River No More: The Colorado River and the West*, Alfred A. Knopf: New York, 1981.

Ghiglieri, Michael P., *First Through Grand Canyon: The Secret Journals and Letters of the 1869 Crew Who Explored the Green and Colorado Rivers*, Puma Press: Flagstaff, 2003.

Porter, Eliot, *The Place No One Knew: Glen Canyon on the Colorado*, Gibbs Smith: Salt Lake City, 2000.

Powell, John Wesley, *The Exploration of the Colorado River and Its Canyons*, National Geographic Press: Washington, D.C., 2002.

Watkins, T. H., *The Grand Colorado: The Story of a River and Its Canyons*, American West Publishing, 1969.

Worster, Donald, *A River Running West: The Life of John Wesley Powell*. Oxford University Press: New York, 2001.

INDEX

AUTHOR'S NOTE

⊢•◆•○•◆•⊣

The photographs on pages 7, 21, 24, and 30 were taken
by John K. Hillers, who was with Powell on his later surveys of
the Colorado River and its canyons. His stunning photographs,
among the best taken of the American West, were even more
remarkable considering the conditions under which they were
created. Photography was in its infancy and equipment was
bulky. Hillers needed two pack horses to haul a 1,000 pounds of
equipment up perilous canyon trails to take a single shot!

More than 400 of John K. Hiller's photographs
can be seen, and downloaded in high resolution, on
the United States Geological Survey's website:
http://libraryphoto.er.usgs.gov/startlib1.htm.
Go to *Pioneer Photographers,* and then *JK Hillers*